De-Compress

Your Stress

Doodle and Draw

Write and Release

De-Compress

Your Stress

Doodle and Draw

Write and Release

By: Dr. Lisa H. Fuller

DeCompress Your Stress
Doodle and Draw
Write and Release

Published by Learn Realistic Habits for the Future
Roseville, MI, USA
www.LearnRealisticHabitsfortheFuture.com

Printed in the United States of America.

Interior & book cover design: Dr. Lisa H. Fuller

ISBN 13: 979-8-9886371-7-2

DISCLAIMER

De-Compress Your Stress, Doodle and Draw, Write and Release does not represent any diagnosis, treatment, recommendations, or advice.

If going through this book precipitates any triggers, flashbacks, emotional responses, etc., contact and follow up with mental and/or medical health professionals. If you are a threat to yourself or others, contact 911 or 988. 988 is a 24-hour Suicide and Crisis Lifeline. *(No affiliations with 911 or 988 exists.)*

Stop reading and working through De-Compress Your Stress, Doodle and Draw, Write and Release if you do not accept all parts of this disclaimer.

This book does not promise any guarantees. You acknowledge you are soley responsibile for your choices and the results received from this book.

This book does not give mental health or medical advice or recommendations.

This book does not provide any legal or financial advice.

PREFACE

Stress can be caused by multiple factors. Life stressors include but are not limited to...

    (1) **Work Stress:** A new job, job termination, lay off, project deadlines, learning a new skill set, conflict with management, hostile work environment, being overlooked for a promotion, or burnout.
    (2) **School Stress:** Test taking, new school environment, peer pressure, conflict with the teacher/ instructor, or difficulty learning the material.
    (3) **Family Life:** Marital discord, financial difficulty, single parenting, and domestic violence.

Not all stress is bad, such as adjusting to being newlyweds or the birth of a new baby. Good stress, such as project deadlines, can prompt alertness or urgency to meet and complete deadlines, which increases productivity.

Each person reacts to and manages stress differently. The impact of stress varies depending on exposure to stress, its intensity, and how one copes with or manages stress.

Picture a high-quality sheet of paper towel with me. You are holding the paper towel on opposite sides using both hands. The paper towel is directly placed under a slow, continuous stream of water. Tension is placed on the paper towel. As the amount of time the paper towel is exposed to the water (exposure to the stressor) and the pressure of the water becomes stronger (intensity of the stressor), the paper towel collapses and falls apart. Your hands will not be able to provide the necessary support to prevent the paper towel from falling apart. Additional support may be needed.

Stress can produce similar results in one's life, especially when there are limited support systems to reduce, remove, or stop stressors. The impact of stress over time can be destabilizing in many ways. Symptoms can manifest physically, mentally, and/or behaviorally.

Manifestations of physical stress can present as headaches, GI/digestion problems, muscle tension, muscle aches and pains, chest pain, rapid heart rate, palpitations, rapid breathing, and fatigue for example. Please note: It is always advisable to seek medical attention when experiencing such concerns.

Manifestations of mental stress can present as depression, anxiety (feelings of being overwhelmed, worrying, panic), irritability, anger, helplessness, interrupted concentration, and sleep disturbance.

Manifestations of behavioral stress can present as sexual promiscuity, addictions, and emotional eating.

When the body perceives a threat, the sympathetic nervous system is activated, triggering the "fight or flight" response, which is one of early man's basic primordial survival skills. The fight or flight response is the body's response to a real or perceived threat or challenge.

Journaling, doodling, drawing, free writing, or any activity that one enjoys and does not find threatening or challenging can be relaxing and fun. In threatening, non-intimidating, or non-challenging environments, the parasympathetic nervous system has the opportunity to restore balance, homeostasis, and calmness.

HOW TO USE THIS BOOK

Draw!   Doodle!   Free write!   Have fun!

Don't worry about punctuation, grammar, or spelling.

Keep De-Compress Your Stress, Doodle and Draw, Write and Release in your desk, car dashboard, nightstand, computer case, or purse.

Take it with you while waiting to board a plane...

During your flight...

Waiting for your doctor or dentist appointment...

During a boring meeting...

On a long road trip...

While your children take a nap...

During a soothing bath...

Whenever you want to take a break.

De-Compress Your Stress
Doodle & Draw

De-Compress Your Stress
Write to Release

_____

_____

_____

_____

_____

_____

_____

_____

_____

_____

_____

_____

_____

_____

_____

_____

_____

_____

_____

_____

_____

_____

De-Compress Your Stress
Doodle & Draw

De-Compress Your Stress
Write to Release

_____

_____

_____

_____

_____

_____

_____

_____

_____

_____

_____

_____

_____

_____

_____

_____

_____

_____

_____

_____

_____

_____

_____

De-Compress Your Stress
Doodle & Draw

De-Compress Your Stress
Write to Release

_____

_____

_____

_____

_____

_____

_____

_____

_____

_____

_____

_____

_____

_____

_____

_____

_____

_____

_____

_____

_____

_____

De-Compress Your Stress
Doodle & Draw

De-Compress Your Stress
Write to Release

_____

_____

_____

_____

_____

_____

_____

_____

_____

_____

_____

_____

_____

_____

_____

_____

_____

_____

_____

_____

_____

_____

_____

De-Compress Your Stress
Doodle & Draw

De-Compress Your Stress
Write to Release

_____

_____

_____

_____

_____

_____

_____

_____

_____

_____

_____

_____

_____

_____

_____

_____

_____

_____

_____

_____

_____

_____

De-Compress Your Stress
Doodle & Draw

De-Compress Your Stress
Write to Release

_____

_____

_____

_____

_____

_____

_____

_____

_____

_____

_____

_____

_____

_____

_____

_____

_____

_____

_____

_____

_____

_____

_____

_____

De-Compress Your Stress
Doodle & Draw

De-Compress Your Stress
Write to Release

_____

_____

_____

_____

_____

_____

_____

_____

_____

_____

_____

_____

_____

_____

_____

_____

_____

_____

_____

_____

_____

De-Compress Your Stress
Doodle & Draw

De-Compress Your Stress
Write to Release

De-Compress Your Stress
Doodle & Draw

De-Compress Your Stress
Write to Release

_____

_____

_____

_____

_____

_____

_____

_____

_____

_____

_____

_____

_____

_____

_____

_____

_____

_____

_____

_____

_____

_____

De-Compress Your Stress
Doodle & Draw

De-Compress Your Stress
Write to Release

_____

_____

_____

_____

_____

_____

_____

_____

_____

_____

_____

_____

_____

_____

_____

_____

_____

_____

_____

_____

_____

_____

_____

_____

_____

De-Compress Your Stress
Doodle & Draw

De-Compress Your Stress
Write to Release

_____

_____

_____

_____

_____

_____

_____

_____

_____

_____

_____

_____

_____

_____

_____

_____

_____

_____

_____

_____

_____

_____

_____

De-Compress Your Stress
Doodle & Draw

De-Compress Your Stress
Write to Release

_____

_____

_____

_____

_____

_____

_____

_____

_____

_____

_____

_____

_____

_____

_____

_____

_____

_____

_____

_____

_____

_____

_____

De-Compress Your Stress
Doodle & Draw

De-Compress Your Stress
Write to Release

_____

_____

_____

_____

_____

_____

_____

_____

_____

_____

_____

_____

_____

_____

_____

_____

_____

_____

_____

_____

_____

_____

De-Compress Your Stress
Doodle & Draw

De-Compress Your Stress
Write to Release

_____

_____

_____

_____

_____

_____

_____

_____

_____

_____

_____

_____

_____

_____

_____

_____

_____

_____

_____

_____

_____

_____

De-Compress Your Stress
Doodle & Draw

De-Compress Your Stress
Write to Release

_____

_____

_____

_____

_____

_____

_____

_____

_____

_____

_____

_____

_____

_____

_____

_____

_____

_____

_____

_____

_____

_____

_____

De-Compress Your Stress
Doodle & Draw

De-Compress Your Stress
Write to Release

_____

_____

_____

_____

_____

_____

_____

_____

_____

_____

_____

_____

_____

_____

_____

_____

_____

_____

_____

_____

_____

_____

_____

De-Compress Your Stress
Doodle & Draw

De-Compress Your Stress
Write to Release

_____

_____

_____

_____

_____

_____

_____

_____

_____

_____

_____

_____

_____

_____

_____

_____

_____

_____

_____

_____

_____

_____

_____

De-Compress Your Stress
Doodle & Draw

De-Compress Your Stress
Write to Release

_____

_____

_____

_____

_____

_____

_____

_____

_____

_____

_____

_____

_____

_____

_____

_____

_____

_____

_____

_____

_____

_____

De-Compress Your Stress
Doodle & Draw

De-Compress Your Stress
Write to Release

_____

_____

_____

_____

_____

_____

_____

_____

_____

_____

_____

_____

_____

_____

_____

_____

_____

_____

_____

_____

_____

_____

De-Compress Your Stress
Doodle & Draw

De-Compress Your Stress
Write to Release

_____

_____

_____

_____

_____

_____

_____

_____

_____

_____

_____

_____

_____

_____

_____

_____

_____

_____

_____

_____

_____

_____

_____

_____

De-Compress Your Stress
Doodle & Draw

De-Compress Your Stress
Write to Release

_____

_____

_____

_____

_____

_____

_____

_____

_____

_____

_____

_____

_____

_____

_____

_____

_____

_____

_____

_____

_____

_____

_____

De-Compress Your Stress
Doodle & Draw

De-Compress Your Stress
Write to Release

_____

_____

_____

_____

_____

_____

_____

_____

_____

_____

_____

_____

_____

_____

_____

_____

_____

_____

_____

_____

_____

De-Compress Your Stress
Doodle & Draw

De-Compress Your Stress
Write to Release

_____

_____

_____

_____

_____

_____

_____

_____

_____

_____

_____

_____

_____

_____

_____

_____

_____

_____

_____

_____

_____

_____

_____

De-Compress Your Stress
Doodle & Draw

De-Compress Your Stress
Write to Release

_____

_____

_____

_____

_____

_____

_____

_____

_____

_____

_____

_____

_____

_____

_____

_____

_____

_____

_____

_____

_____

_____

_____

De-Compress Your Stress
Doodle & Draw

De-Compress Your Stress
Write to Release

_____

_____

_____

_____

_____

_____

_____

_____

_____

_____

_____

_____

_____

_____

_____

_____

_____

_____

_____

_____

_____

_____

_____

De-Compress Your Stress
Doodle & Draw

De-Compress Your Stress
Write to Release

_____

_____

_____

_____

_____

_____

_____

_____

_____

_____

_____

_____

_____

_____

_____

_____

_____

_____

_____

_____

_____

_____

_____

_____

De-Compress Your Stress
Doodle & Draw

De-Compress Your Stress
Write to Release

De-Compress Your Stress
Doodle & Draw

De-Compress Your Stress
Write to Release

_____

_____

_____

_____

_____

_____

_____

_____

_____

_____

_____

_____

_____

_____

_____

_____

_____

_____

_____

_____

_____

_____

De-Compress Your Stress
Doodle & Draw

De-Compress Your Stress
Write to Release

_____

_____

_____

_____

_____

_____

_____

_____

_____

_____

_____

_____

_____

_____

_____

_____

_____

_____

_____

_____

_____

_____

_____

De-Compress Your Stress
Doodle & Draw

De-Compress Your Stress
Write to Release

_____

_____

_____

_____

_____

_____

_____

_____

_____

_____

_____

_____

_____

_____

_____

_____

_____

_____

_____

_____

_____

_____

De-Compress Your Stress
Doodle & Draw

De-Compress Your Stress
Write to Release

_____

_____

_____

_____

_____

_____

_____

_____

_____

_____

_____

_____

_____

_____

_____

_____

_____

_____

_____

_____

_____

_____

De-Compress Your Stress
Doodle & Draw

De-Compress Your Stress
Write to Release

_____

_____

_____

_____

_____

_____

_____

_____

_____

_____

_____

_____

_____

_____

_____

_____

_____

_____

_____

_____

_____

_____

_____

De-Compress Your Stress
Doodle & Draw

De-Compress Your Stress
Write to Release

_____

_____

_____

_____

_____

_____

_____

_____

_____

_____

_____

_____

_____

_____

_____

_____

_____

_____

_____

_____

_____

_____

_____

De-Compress Your Stress
Doodle & Draw

De-Compress Your Stress
Write to Release

_____

_____

_____

_____

_____

_____

_____

_____

_____

_____

_____

_____

_____

_____

_____

_____

_____

_____

_____

_____

_____

_____

_____

_____

De-Compress Your Stress
Doodle & Draw

De-Compress Your Stress
Write to Release

De-Compress Your Stress
Doodle & Draw

De-Compress Your Stress
Write to Release

_____

_____

_____

_____

_____

_____

_____

_____

_____

_____

_____

_____

_____

_____

_____

_____

_____

_____

_____

_____

_____

De-Compress Your Stress
Doodle & Draw

De-Compress Your Stress
Write to Release

_____

_____

_____

_____

_____

_____

_____

_____

_____

_____

_____

_____

_____

_____

_____

_____

_____

_____

_____

_____

_____

_____

_____

De-Compress Your Stress
Doodle & Draw

De-Compress Your Stress
Write to Release

De-Compress Your Stress
Doodle & Draw

De-Compress Your Stress
Write to Release

_____

_____

_____

_____

_____

_____

_____

_____

_____

_____

_____

_____

_____

_____

_____

_____

_____

_____

_____

_____

_____

_____

_____

_____

_____

De-Compress Your Stress
Doodle & Draw

De-Compress Your Stress
Write to Release

_____

_____

_____

_____

_____

_____

_____

_____

_____

_____

_____

_____

_____

_____

_____

_____

_____

_____

_____

_____

_____

_____

De-Compress Your Stress
Doodle & Draw

De-Compress Your Stress
Write to Release

_____

_____

_____

_____

_____

_____

_____

_____

_____

_____

_____

_____

_____

_____

_____

_____

_____

_____

_____

_____

_____

_____

_____

De-Compress Your Stress
Doodle & Draw

De-Compress Your Stress
Write to Release

De-Compress Your Stress
Doodle & Draw

De-Compress Your Stress
Write to Release

_____

_____

_____

_____

_____

_____

_____

_____

_____

_____

_____

_____

_____

_____

_____

_____

_____

_____

_____

_____

_____

_____

_____

ABOUT THE AUTHOR

For more than 30 years, Dr. Lisa H. Fuller has practiced psychiatry and provided mental health awareness and training in the greater Detroit area and surrounding states including Ohio, Indiana, and West Virginia. Dr. Lisa H. Fuller is the CEO and CMO of Discern Life Consultants Health. She has led mission teams on the continents of Africa, Asia, Europe, and North America (including Panama and the United States), with a focus on crisis, trauma, leadership development, and spirituality.

Second Ebenezer Church/ Bishop Edgar L. Vann recognized Dr. Fuller for Outstanding Leadership in Global Missions. The Liberian Evangelical Baptist Convention in Ganta, Liberia presented Dr. Fuller with the Distinguished Servanthood Honor. The Rapid Response Chaplain Corps presented Dr. Fuller with a Master Teacher and Humanitarian Award. Articles written on Dr. Lisa H. Fuller appear in Speakers Magazine, US Times, New York Business Now, and Women's Journal.

Academic appointments include Assistant Professor Wayne State University School of Medicine/ Department of Psychiatry and Behavioral Neurosciences/ Emergency Psychiatry, Guest Professor/ Bulgaria Ecumenical Theological Seminary (Sofia, Bulgaria), Guest Professor DayStar University/ Department of Psychology/ Crisis & Trauma, and Instructor Destiny School of Ministry. Keynote and featured speaking assignments include U.S. Army Corps of Engineers, Nairobi Women's Hospital/Gender Violence Unit (Nairobi, Kenya), and Global Projects Hope, Help, Healing.

Dr. Fuller is the Founder and Overseer for Lisa H. Fuller Ministries, Christ's Arms Reaching Everywhere Ministries, Learn Realistic Habits for the Future publishing company and host of a six-year running radio broadcast, "A Word of Encouragement," in Cincinnati, Ohio, Southeast Indiana, and Northern Kentucky. You can purchase Dr. Fuller's books on Amazon and wherever books are sold.

To Contact Dr. Lisa H. Fuller Visit:

https://DrLisaHFuller.com/
https://LisaHFullerMinistries.org/
https://ChristsArmsReachingEverywhere.org/
https://LearnRealisticHabitsForTheFuture.com
https://DiscernLifeConsultants.com/

MENTAL HEALTH/ ENCOURAGEMENT

Books By Dr. Lisa H. Fuller

DEVOTIONAL & ENCOURAGEMENT

Books By Dr. Lisa H. Fuller

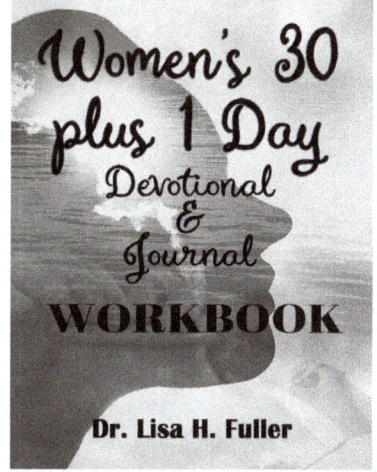

DEVOTIONAL & ENCOURAGEMENT

Books By Dr. Lisa H. Fuller

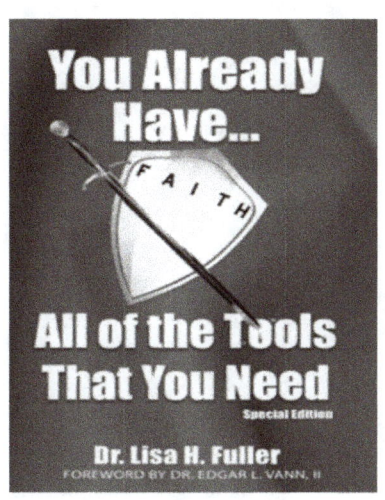

MISSIONS PLANNING & INSTRUCTION

Books By Dr. Lisa H. Fuller

www.ingramcontent.com/pod-product-compliance
Lightning Source LLC
Chambersburg PA
CBHW061701120626
46550CB00003B/1042